Falling Blues sings about edges and air,
go, jumping, plunging. The poems chai
ways we have of falling in and out (of lo
for and under (spells, sinners, mystics), c
and getting back up and on again. It`s a.
carries us, what we are given, what we learn and what — and who
— we take with us on the vertiginous journey through the body`s
mischief, to the stillness we imagine lies beyond falling.

Also by Jannie Edwards:

The Possibilities of Thirst (1997)
Blood Opera: The Raven Tango Poems (2006)

Falling Blues

Jannie Edwards

Frontenac House
Calgary, Alberta

Book and cover design: Epix Design
Cover Image: From "True Stories" by Constanza Pacher
Author photo: Paul Saturley

Library and Archives Canada Cataloguing in Publication

Edwards, Jannie, 1951-
    Falling blues / Jannie Edwards.

Poems.
ISBN 978-1-897181-36-2

    I. Title.

PS8559.D855F35 2010   C811'.54   C2009-907345-5

We acknowledge the support of the Canada Council for the Arts for our
publishing program and the support of the Alberta Creative Development
Initiative. We also acknowledge the support of The Alberta Foundation for
the Arts.

Canada Council   Conseil des Arts
for the Arts   du Canada

Alberta
Foundation
for the Arts

Printed and bound in Canada
Published by Frontenac House Ltd.
1138 Frontenac Avenue S.W.
Calgary, Alberta, T2T 1B6, Canada
Tel: 403-245-2491 Fax: 403-245-2380
editor@frontenachouse.com   www.frontenachouse.com

for my youngest and oldest teachers

Beatrice Alma Edwards

and

David Boaz Gottshall

Acknowledgements

Earlier versions of poems were published in the following: *dANDdelion*, *Freefall*, *Other Voices*, *The Fiddlehead*, *Arc* and *Grain*.

"Blues for the Blues" was published in *Why I Sing the Blues* (Smoking Lung, 2001, edited by Jan Zwicky and Brad Cran) and *Jane Austen Sings the Blues* (University of Alberta Press, 2008, edited by Nora Stovel).

"In Praise of Tending" was published in in *Waging Peace: Poetry and Political Action* (Penumbra Press, 2002, edited by Susan McMaster) and reprinted in *Imagine a World: Poetry for Peacemakers* (PAX Christi USA, 2005) edited by Peggy Rosenthal.

"I Have Five Things To Say" is a homage to Rumi.

The line "… enrolled in Doomsday, waiting for parole" in "The Future" is adapted from Hafiz.

The shades of blue in "Martha Stewart's Tips on Cultivating Melancholia" are inspired by Don McKay, used with permission from the author.

The epigraphs in "Anemographia: Some Species of Wind" are from John Thompson's *Stilt Jack*, "Ghazals V and VI" in *John Thompson: Collected Poems and Translations*, edited by Peter Sanger. Fredricton, NB: Goose Lane Editions, 1995.

The quotations in "What We Mean When We Say Love" are from *Like Gold in the Fire: Voices of Hope from El Salvador: War, Exile and Return 1974-1999*. Nottingham, UK: Nueva Esperanza Support Group, 1999. The first quotation is by Armando, a guerrilla fighter in the El Salvador war; the second is by Mina Fernandez.

"Luck" is for David Gottshall.

"the way between them" is for Darci and Mel Mallon.

"Water Road" is for Marlene Stewart.

My deepest thanks to all those who helped shape these poems – you know who you are – especially to Catherine Owen.

Gratitude to all my great teachers, especially Little Bea and Big David. For my parents, Denise de Chazal (1909-1976) and George Stafford-Mayer (1909-1991). Mark, as always, in love, squalor and mind meld; and to daughters Merryn, Caitlin and Rhiannon, who keep me honest.

Contents

Still Life

Falling Blues

I Have Five Things to Say

First, there is no shame in being lost.

Second, learn how to fall.

Third, when you found me, I was waiting.

Fourth, forget how to count!

Fifth, I am a slow learner.
It took me half a life to learn
the bowl must sometimes be empty.
Now, I must learn about the bowl breaking.

Carrying Charges

You know these things as thoughts, but your thoughts are not your experiences, they are an echo and an after-effect of your experiences, as when your room trembles when a carriage goes past. I, however, am sitting in the carriage, and often I am the carriage itself.

Friedrich Nietzsche, *Thus Spoke Zarathustra*

Calling

Sleep is stubborn tonight.
The day a gristled lump,
repeating itself.

Listening to the old dog
lap lap lap lap
at the toilet bowl oasis.
When does it stop being *never too late?*

Then without warning
I'm blindsided, locked
in a fisted dream,
painting a door
in the brunted cell of my life.

On the other side, the X
carved in a map of sand dreams
You are here.

Sand dreams rock, harbour.
Harbour dreams horizon.
Rock, catapult

and I'm hurled through the door
into the roaring chassis of the desert
into the middle of a dire voice that drills

Strip. Burn. Change.

Occupation

1.

In the old photograph, my mother poses on her honeymoon
with a bevy of beautiful young German men. Germany, summer
1938. Her face, soft with love, looks straight into her new
husband's camera. From London to paddle down the Rhine,
their kayak is pulled up on shore, two paddles hold open the
flaps of their canvas pup tent. My mother is in the centre. The
gorgeous youths around her exude privilege, choice breeding.
They have bared their torsos, knotted scarves elegantly around
their necks. The one closest to my mother has his legs tucked
languidly, his arm draping another man's shoulders. Six are
smiling – two sweet, four ironic. Two not smiling. They are all
lustrous with health, their muscles easy, ready.

2.

Four picture-perfect columns of Hitler Jügend are marching,
boots up to their calves, woollen jackets buckled smartly in spite
of the summer heat. Uniform height, no nonsense faces, even
though it's the wine festival, the harvest is in and the street is
festive with bunting, everyone in their Sunday best. Two girls
at the edge are costumed like wenches. One smiles shyly at
the camera. The young men hoist shovels like guns over their
shoulders.

3.

What do I want from these old photographs? That my parents
were beautiful lovers on Wagnerian rivers, consorting with
would-be officers as the machinery of evil collected itself
with cool devotion? That they survived? It is the end of the
millennium, the stories are piling up, the long backward glance.
We know there are too many ways to die, that the lucky die their
(*please* my, our) own deaths, that there are only a few ways to love,
that to love the hard way is delicate and violent, that we can
count on only a very few to go that hard way with us.

4.

The Holocaust changes everything, says Ruth, child of a child
survivor. *Everything: the way you eat, make love, inhabit your body,
the way you are occupied.* The way when you began to piece your
father's story, how being outside of the story you were inside of
all along turned you inside out. The way you attend fiercely to
ghosts, fiercely to the imagination of evil. Just when you think
you've seen it all, another headline screams: a school smeared
with swastikas, firebombed. The way your story has gotten inside
me. The way no one is let off
the hook.

Elegy for My Last Aunt

My last aunt – gone. And with her the faith
That harm, its clodding thuggery, its abattoir
Boots, could be checked, even disgraced
By exact cutlery, precise ankles, fixtures
Of the old charm school nostrums, their tropes.
With every channel now a melee of crotch
And heave, half-lives of desire: Super Gulp
Glug glug, self-serve cruise control ratcheted
Up so far beyond Aunt Lily's help or reach.
And worse. The gyre churning, enraptured
By its spin. Outsourced torture. Preachers
Spurred by revenge, caballed with butchers.
Dear Aunt, through all you held fast
To gentility, fierce and gentle to the last.

The Girl with Cold Hands

She had such cold hands. She dated the boy with the thick neck
who went down by the river with his buddies. They took the girl
who wasn't too bright – the girl with the flower name: Daisy?
Rose? Those boys had their fun with her. They got off in the
trial and the girl with the flower name, her hair fell out in big
clumps. What nobody knew was while all this was going on, the
girl with cold hands was in the family way, knocked up, up the
stump. The girl whose cold hands tingled through my thin slip,
taking my measurements in grade eight Home Ec. The sensible
one. The one the teacher got to write all our measurements on
the board for everyone to see: bust, waist, hips. She married the
boy with the thick neck the summer after high school graduation,
the summer after the trial. Sewed her own wedding dress and
all her bridesmaids' dresses, carefully measuring the white satin,
pink crepe, high Empire waists. So good in math. So good with
her hands.

Let's say the boy with the thick neck was called Les.
Let's say he liked to let 'er rip.
Let's say he knew better.
Let's say the girl whose hair fell out was called Violet.
Let's say she got a job at the confectionary.
Let's say she got on with everyone like a house on fire, was a real
cut up.
Let's say they called the baby Frank.
Let's say he grew up to become an actuary, calculating premium
rates, dividends, risks.
Let's say the girl with cold hands coaxed hothouse roses to bloom
on the prairies.
Let's say Angela.
Let's just say her name.

Carrying Charges

The girl-woman, parked
at the food court table, stares
at a baby close by.
Doubled over, she grins, drools,
her round face a cartoon moon dangling
over her lap.

The baby stares back.
Don't touch, warns the girl's keeper.
She obeys. Slumps on the cramped chair,
her body yeasty as a grandmother's.
But her voice,
the voice in her gut will not sit still.

She flings sound out to the baby
Ma Ma
a bright plaything   *Ma Ma*
India rubber ball, taut
on its paddle-tethered string
Aaaghh   Ma Ma

The baby is unmoved,
a small Buddha.
The mother reads, her idle hand rocking
the stroller.
Revved up now, the girl hurls sound,
More, more, screams
Ma Ma   Aaaghh

Unbearable, she is dragged away
wailing down the mall: *Shush, shush.*

Oh, that slow fadeout of grief –
longing crammed
into the caged machine of voice,
its gunned, broken idiom.

Fiat Flux

for L. Cohen

Your nettled psalms sting, Leonard,
they squeeze us to our knees
in this unholy bout of history.
We can't get enough, we're spent,

Hell bent, undone
by the way you unclock Doom and Love,
Dance Misery!
flume their sprung nerves through the reeling ruins
of brokenness. A kind of salve.

Ten-thousand foundered pilgrims,
rife and vertiginous in the Jumbotroned Epoch
of Post-Traumatic Irony, all of us falling,
Sing Angels!
grateful, into the wake of your tidal tow.

Praise be a working man.

Anemographia: Some Species of Wind

1.

> *What darkens*
> *the winds we don't understand?*
> John Thompson, *Stilt Jack*

A slurred wind, rehearsing its rut.

A tomcat skunk wind, a punk spray wind that torques **KEEP OUT** to **KEEP SHOUTING.**

Death's knife wind afflicting the whittled house with homelessness.

A rictus wind, unmustered, sick.

A windigo blizzard wind riddling double-tongued glosses on the hunger of ice.

A grief wind, grave-heavy gibbet wind, sadness so thick you can brand it.

A troying wind rumouring loved ones, keening for home.

2.

anger
dies with the wind.

A suffing young nurse wind stroking her night rounds, smoothing open soft windows.

A suckling spring wind, all mouth, rooting among the sticky nipple-fisted poplar buds.

A crack-fingered, wit-stealing, *prima mobile* mainspring Houdini trick wind: *Poof!*
Whatever you're clutching – gone.

An amnesty wind that springs all your charges into song.

The Hunger Artist

The beautiful anorexics
caught freaked
across the tabloids' catwalk
tweak for me Kafka's
Hunger Artist, that radical
philosopher of greed
and sadness who bought
his audiences breakfast
then watched them eat.
I want to read Kafka's story
with those lovely tabloid ghosts,
this primer on performing
the wonders of starvation
for the crowds of locust eyes,
mouths obese with grease
pressed restless against
the glass cage.

Do you remember cooling it
in the grocery lineups, scanning
the headlines in the *Weekly World News,*
smiling at the clumsy lurid photos:
Bat Boy, aliens mating with humans,
Nostradamus' encryptions
about the end of the world.
When was it we noticed that Elvis
had pretty much finally left the building
for good, let go, at long last, resuscitated
only on death anniversaries:
Elvis Lives as Elvis Impersonator in Ohio.

At the height of his fame
the Hunger Artist's impresario
scripted the show so that after
forty days and nights
two titillated young ladies

favoured by drawn lot
would lead him from his cell
draped on their shoulders
through the crowd
to the hospital meal
while the doctors hovered
and the military band blustered,
mustering the crowd.
Thin as a saint's razor,
sensitive as a new burn,
the Hunger Artist struggled
to explain his art
to those with no feeling
for it. Eventually,
the rabble got bored
with watching him die
slowly. They charged by, bent
on the caged animals.
The Hunger Artist was replaced
by a panther.

I miss the *Weekly World News*
in the grocery lineups, its crazy ludicrousness:
Dwarf Trains to be Astronaut in Dryer;
Flea Circus Goes Wild with Hunger, Attacks Trainer.
It was more fun than this queasy celebrity parade
of betrayal and booty, the creepy vaunting
of weight, the gawkish vampirism
around the heft and the absence of women's flesh,
breakups, breakdowns.

What would the Hunger Artist make of this?
He knew that he was replaceable,
that his was a dying art.
Still, would he marvel
at the way hunger persists,
the way it conscripts us all?

Falling by Stranger

Chen, quivering
on the brink of the Haizhu Bridge, calibrates
a negotiation with gravity.

The drag of his two million yuan debt lugs,
stakes him to the verge. Five hours he blocks traffic,
stranded in a Babel of cell phones, cameras

Until Lai, on his way to the hospital
to refill medication for *mental illness*, breaks through
the police barricade, shakes Chen's hand

and pushes him, saluting the fall.
Selfish, Lai accuses Chen.
A violation of public interest.

Nobody dies. Yet.
An inflatable cushion breaks Chen's fall.
The Pearl River, riddled

with cherry blossoms, carries on.
Traffic resumes. Bystanders brim home,
loaded with spectacle.

There is talk of putting Lai on government retainer.
11 suicide attempts on Haizhu Bridge in April alone.

Read the Air

What are you afraid of, flying girl?

Being tethered, clipped, sweetly towned and gowned,
No space for my signature, just purl, knit, purl,
Counting, counting, down and down and down.
What will I do with all these birds in my head?
Croombing dove in the morning, swooping swallow
At noon. Sometimes a hawk dreams in my bed.
Who knows which I'll follow?
My father warns of gravity, drag.
Mother croons to her pretty caged cockatiels.
My sister, just wed, hoists a flag
Over her mate. A preening pair, wheeling their deal.

Flying girl, don't hurry. Burn
The air. Make it cursive with your yearning.

Luck

You're in the forest with no coat,
no compass, and your only companion is you
and you have a terrible sense of direction.
Fear has ricked your brain into a glass tightrope
and every sound is a hurled rock that just barely
misses. Unbelievably, what riddles your grip there
in the rattled forest is that joke you've heard
maybe a coupla dozen times – the one about the man,
terrified of bears, who finds himself eyeboring
into the death-yellow eyes of a grizzly.
The man's scream balloons out of his throat,
a cartoon genie that shapes into a God-sized prayer
rising like a florid lava-lamp kite past the Gotham head
of the grizzly who's now reared up on his hind legs
ready to eviscerate the man, and this
is the prayer that the man howls:
Please God, let this be a Christian bear.

At this point you feel you can take your time,
remember the way he told it, stretch
the clouds into fanned-out Jesus rays and maybe
there's a simmering chorus of angels while the bear freezes
in mid-primal swipe, petrifies,
scratches his head, then bows to say grace:
Lord, for what I am about to receive, make me truly thankful.

And after you tell yourself this joke again and again,
you might start to lift a little lighter, try a few more turns.
And suddenly you realize
you have always been in the forest
and there has always been a story, a friend,
and the story can be your coat.

Song of Advanced Capitalism

This is the song of excess. The song of desire that won't stop.
A song for all those who have forgotten the secret password for
Cease.

The step-right-up gruntathon of the 24-hour All You Can Eat
buffets, muzak jawing itself into your brain. The flatfooted
waddling song of a hundred tuba players playing for an Old
Tyme pie eating contest in a mall. This is the song of gorge and
binge, of swollen eyes, swollen stomachs.

A song of the lumpenproletariat powered by some strain of
nuclear yeast into orgies of confession, pathos hyperbolized into
bathos and sold over the counter in every convenience store.

The fix song of therapy, the breakdown-stranded-by-the-highway
song, the song of the big black book that promises drugged
rescue, that lists the names of all the diseases of the soul in a
catalogue whose direct mail list, once you sign on to, you can
never get off.

The heaving song of dancing elephants cursed with sequined
g-strings. And the song of those who think this is cute.

The strangled song of the choked heart of the behemoth,
beamed in on every TV satellite dish, the song that craves little
girls with pouty reddened lips and pretend cleavage.

The skinflick song whose tongue flirts with all your itches and
makes them worse.

The bang of the dirigible Pop can blown up, its bits reassembled
in the cannibal song of style.

The long howl, digitally rerecorded, of History's saddest train whistles, the quality of that sound.

The song of war as spectacle.

The *ka-ching ka-ching ka-ching* of VLTs whose lemons never line up.

The glut that eats its own heart out even as it grows back, feeding on nostalgia, 5-kleenex tearjerkers, and bestseller guides to voluntary simplicity.

This is the song whose chorus is the scream of kennelled dogs doing time for a thousand bitches in heat.

This is the so-far-gone song, been-gone-so-long song, it's lost its lungs, its ears, can't breathe or listen to itself, lurches along, all eyes, mouth, gut, groin, its arms outstretched...

Missing

Suddenly at the edge, night
shifts, juddering

and the giant octopus machine of the city recharges
its hundred million concatenations of desire

its prowling brokenness, bad dates
debt service ratio, missed connections

its dirty tricks, call centres
gated enclaves, vanity plates

(Missing)

its bridal fairs, timed exposures
glass masters, asset management

self-serve glutted abattoirs
personal touch obedience schools

its rebar stilettos, direct deposits
service sector, guaranteed results

(Missing)

its risk managers, payday loans
target markets, flat rate fantasies

always open, discreet
bodies of knowledge, injury claims

Listen: again at the edge, night
shifts, a stifled shuddering scream, another

Missing

The Future

January's moon's gone stale.
Weeks stammer their traffic.

The long marriage with weather
has us all enrolled in Doomsday, waiting for parole.

In the dream my mother is young again, slim
as still water. The abalone moon trembles

taut as a trampoline in its lack
of gravity. There are no footprints yet.

A hand-stitched trousseau fidgets
in its tissue: *soon, soon.*

My father is hard pressed, studying his biology, his maps.
There will be exams. There will be wars.

"Here I am," I call to those beautiful, ruthless
creatures, my heart racing

against the clock. "Here I am,
your child, your dream."

The Body's Mischief

The body's mischief proceeds from the soul; and if the soul is not satisfied, the body can never be cured.

Robert Burton, *The Anatomy of Melancholy*

Tough Cookie

Dare

At six, she prickled *dare* in us like a rash – *C'mon!*
But only she hurtled off the edge
of the roof, her small frog body a nerve
hitting the trampoline, arcing *lift*
again and again,
while the rest of us huddled in the baby pool
up to our necks in water tepid
as pee, squinting at the sky.
She'd try anything once.
Stole nail polish, siren red, later
a whole frozen chicken stuffed down her pants.
Twenty bucks ripped off from her mother's purse
bought us all Dairy Queen.
Her posse, she called us.
Flattery. We were farm fair gawkers,
her audience. Only she had quick-draw
trigger instincts, sprung
for the high wire.

Surely, she was bound for sex early.
Jumped up little Columbus
freebooting through the city going
down down going
down
        coming back
with such strange tales
of the barbarians.

Nerve

She was a tough little cookie, hard case.
Wisecrack body itching
to sucker punch the last word
      What're you lookin at?
Black-rimmed eyes glaring,
legs bared in winter, cornered
in that too-small frozen town, flaunting
her bad reputation.

When the wrestler Sweet Daddy Siki came to town,
skin like milk chocolate,
bleached hair fake as a three-dollar bill,
he schticked his sweet time sauntering in the spotlight,
cooing to a mirror in each hand
      the ladies pet and the men fret
sliding up to pounding
the crap outta the other guy.

Well,
she made him look.

What did he see?
A skinny white girl, pressed tight
up against the ring,
anxious to say yes to anything.

What did she see?
Pure nerve.
A blacksilver curve carving
the edge of dare.
And her veins,
small taut rivers tensed
for the ice to break free.

My Mother's Laugh

She wasn't like the other 1950s mothers their epiphanies
of ironing casserole recipes painted-on red lips matching
pocketbooks girdled chafing dishes

Me a peeled snail blushing under her schoolyard summons *Coo-ee
Darling! Over here!*

Hooting off her mistake sporting two different coloured pumps
to the Ladies Aid Strawberry Tea where *Mrs. Boomer poured for the
first hour*

She taught me *mouli mai* – Créole from her childhood – *mouli mai,*
when you're so frightened your sphincter clenches hard enough
to grind corn

Laughter collecting in the deep generator of my mother's belly
teasing me out from behind stormy pouts her arms open wide

Come child

my balsam head surfing jelly laughwaves on her yeasty belly
pillow her negligee rippling like the blue of resurrection my ear a
raft alive to her belly borborigmia ruckus riffing *viva voce* ballyhoo
jubilee rollicking dolphin leaps

Come child

Kissing

My mother told me
Don't kiss a boy on the lips unless you mean business.

So

boy i got busy coming to grips with lips on the sin bus
of buzziness   running laps around the lips of busy boys
i was bussing flips dips working up a mean steam
gleaning the boyness of the kissing bizness
minnow tongues slick with silvered slivers
shivered chivaree ooo boy!
don't undress a kiss unless you mean to confess
lean into the soft messy sweet breathy deftness
busy boy frisk those hot lips at the door c'mon kiss me
around the bend over the edge
kiss me into *lift*
kiss me falling into All

The Way

The Sleepover Girls

Giddy from dancing hard in each other's orbits
truth   dare   double dare   promise to repeat
they've gone incandescent from risk
in the bright city their dancing makes.

Girls, their bodies making strange
on them, dress up, invent concoctions
of whatwillbe grownup, as winged out
as the idea of sex, its fractal weirdness.

The sleepover girls suck the juice
from swearwords: cactus cocktail,
and not my shouts, not the shouts of the father
can stop the artesian giggling in these girls.

When midnight pools around their basement nest,
one by one, reluctant, girls surrender to sleep.
See how they've curled around
each other, a fist of petals.

That Girl

That girl. Who writes about bicycles and communist landlords
and sleeping spooned around her Polish grandmother.

Whose mind buzzes with lives and whole cities,
charting the archipelagos of desire. That girl.

Whose sister cut her long brown hair
then said, *I screwed up. You look like Stephen Hawking.*

Who perches in her body at parties like a sparrow,
fibrillating in swarms of secrets. That girl.

Who works the drone till at Liquidation World,
calibrates the charged bargain of her life

And won't flip *Have a nice day* at strangers.
Instead, grins her crooked gap-toothed Esperanto.

That girl whose heart is a depth sonar
scoring its overtime torque. I love that girl.

Rita MacNeil's Feet

                startle me, naked
as a blurted secret, shocking
as seeing your aunt's breasts, loose
as a moon-faced confession.

Just there, in the National Library foyer,
her feet framed in a lineup of photographs:
Famous Canadians, artfully arranged.

They seem shy as come-upon deer, but
mounted somehow, fixed as Victorian taxidermy.
I want to coax them out
from behind the dark frame
and say, Rita, let's waltz away
from here, let's waltz

away to Babylon where we'll splash
in the river with the holy unholy ones.
And you'll honey the melody like a run
of good luck, like you do, Rita,
like you do, and we'll sing
Magdalena, Magdalena,
soft as willows, plump as pillows—

Howcouldya refuse me, Rita, howcouldya?

Emily Dickinson on the Prairies, August

they would have tidalwaved you your lace-encrusted life
weathervaned: loaded   charged   so charged for conversion
that when a circus passed by your window you tasted RED in
your brain

o emily slim alchemist who made prairie from a single clover a
solitary bee   imagine the full assault of sky and land rushing
your upstairs window   rendering your lace curtain a small white
flag hoisting your inland soul through high seas of libertine
wheat bumpertobullionbumper groundswelling into deep
eternity past blue flax prodigal as sky in golden fields   past wads
of brown-eyed susans highrolling in ditches amber dragonflies
everywhere and the wind god the wind such a lover whisper gust
breeze blast squall half a gale fullblown storm tornado
Wild days! Wild days!

and the nights –
late summer night nips as we lurch over the swell of hill to rock
on our blanketed backs and squander awe on the night sky
run to seed with stars   how some nights simmer until about
midnight then
Lightning Thunder Hueandcry some fine Evangelical
Hullabaloo

Done with the compass! Done with the chart!

emily, it was you who taught me prairie:
how water is taught by thirst
harvest, by drought
birds, by snow

Martha Stewart's Tips
on Cultivating Melancholia

Collect certain shades of blue. See the poet's catalogue: puréed cello, distant hills, forgetfulness coming up for air.

Peel off your socks after six months of hard winter. Inspect your feet.

Keep a log of the moon in its most perverse incarnations. Moon, March 13th: a hydrocephalic child's head. Moon, March 19th: torn strip of a wedding dress.

Write *fontanel*.

Plan a road trip through the prairies in January. Drive at night through nearly deserted towns with hopeful names and gawk at the open windows of houses lit up like old-fashioned Christmas cards. Want those lives.

Buy memorial knickknacks in charity thrift shops: for example, a silver plated candy dish engraved *Don & Darlene, 25th Anniversary.*

Read only the poetry of suicides.

Waltz by yourself to old cowboy waltzes, the ones with fiddles that sound like trained coyotes.

Leave. Come back. Shut the door to hear that certain *click* over and over.

Attempt to describe your deepest fears to a telemarketer.

Plan picnics in graveyards, especially by the tombstones of infants. Eat oysters on the half shell and drink milk.

Walk by the sea in a dense fog. Realize that everything that can be known or spoken or imagined has already been.

Enjoy.

March, Edmonton

March petered out like a bad marriage. Like old plumbing.
When he moved out, Winter left his sad trash, too lazy to toss
his mateless gloves and socks, his butts, empty bottles, his tired
old geezer underwear. Spring had to tread gingerly around his
leavings, careful not to slip, so it was like he'd never left.

Spring was feeling worn out herself – strangely light and heavy
at the same time, like a huge dust bunny. Like a bad perm on
an old blonde – brassy and ashen, dusty – like "why bother?"
you know, like the effort was such a waste. Spring felt as if she'd
been around the block too many times, though she hadn't left the
house in weeks.

When Wind careened into town, driving a screaming metallic-
blue Toronado, fully loaded and dangerous, people got edgy.
Gunning his motor at all hours, wailing crazy stuff in the dead
of night, stuff that set your teeth on edge though you couldn't
make out the words.
The good news was that Wind levered Spring out of her fug
like a shoehorn. She'd been sitting on the sagging couch, feeling
weary as her limp bra straps, staring at the bank calendar picture
of April: a virulent carpet of red and yellow tulips somewhere in
B.C., or Venus. The first time she heard Wind's carrying on, she
wept. Not just a good cry. A weep.
When she'd finished, she went on a right rampage: grabbed
some scissors and cut her lank hair, gathered up all the tired
old trash and chucked it; then she scrubbed 'n polished, spit 'n
shined, beat 'n swept, until she'd lathered herself up into a fine
froth like her white sheets whipsnapping on the line, singing scat
duets with Wind.

She ordered herself some new underwear from the Sears
catalogue – daffodil and hyacinth grape and nanking cherry and
lilac. And a new dress, too. Green.

She could hardly wait.

Sprung City

When spring purrs feral
into the city, all traps
are sprung, all bets off

Bus stop boy, red hat,
grooves on bongos while April
fools with snow flurries

At 5th & Jasper
north wind snatches the beggar's cry,
flings it at me: *Change?*

Red light. Top-down Porsche
insists *I can't GET no Sat-is-*
FAC-tion, but I try ...

In the blind alley
a sign beside a prone man –
I'M SLEEPING NOT DEAD

The moon-faced girl on
the packed Number 9 bus
rocks *Ma-ma, Ma-ma*

This is the season
of tabloids: bleeding trees,
escaped wild things

3 a.m.   Outside
my window the café sign, missing
O, neons PEN

Blues for the Blues

Even the blind man knows
When he's walking in the sun.
          ~ B. B. King

What I would give
What I would give
for a horn
in this lonely room

Give to get pulled
through the blue marrow of a climbing slide
pitch its arc
perfectly
to your absence.

What I would give to play the note that pulls
you all the way in.
To do for you what red
does for blue
Go deeper.

Man, what I would give
for you
So long gone
from this lonesome bed
hot
with the midnight blues.

After All

loving you again
after all the brokenness we made

after all the silence we grew
turned to ice, shattered

in the long night
tense as a tourniquet

loving you again
after all

is like finding myself pregnant
after a civil war, stricken

triumphant as blind tubers
in a winter cellar, straining

toward a memory of light

Maud

Maud cocks her ear to the young poet
hears how he haunts elegy, hears the way
gloam and *hoar* coat his tongue, imagines
him rehearsing at the pool of his mirror,
sonorous, deep:
>   *Loss, Loss*

In his poem, the young poet watches himself
by the side of the highway, chronicling light
that registers its long slant on a compass abandoned
in the grass: the burnished moment, its outstretched
sensibilities exquisite,
doomed.

Maud knows scant about nothing but what she's lost
and found. She's the Lonely Planet Guide
to Empty, and the young poet itches her restless
as a northern spring.
It's not that she wishes him
any hard bunkering down,
bouts of rough fixes.
No. She loves his long hair, the minuet of his stroll.

Who knows what she wants.
Perhaps, to tell him:

How spring troubles hunger.
Some species of wind.
The calibrating of fear, hope.

The hankering for an equal
to whisper these decipherings.

Testimony

1. History

Testimony, from the Latin *testis,* witness,
but also cousin to *testis,* testicle.

One theory is that Romans placed their right hands
on their testicles to swear truth
when testifying in court.
Another version has knights pledging fealty
to their lords by grasping their testicles and twisting.
It makes sense, I suppose, to swear on these meek vessels,
small moons, open to wounding blows,
a most tender place to offer obligation.

2. Vision

In a dream I see a field of naked men,
their bodies at ease, penises soft,
their testicles tender as ripe plums.
Over there – a Buddha-bellied man works a garden,
then supines both hands behind his head
and gazes up at a cloud-heaped sky. A slender man,
his head on one arm, one knee slightly bent,
sketches plans for a kitchen or a boat.
A smooth-backed boy turns his head slowly,
his face half shadowed, his eyes full of music.
Everywhere there are dandelions gone to seed.
            No one is alarmed.

These men have been in this field so long
they have forgotten what they were waiting for,
their urgencies settled by a weight like absence or snow.
I have no urge to paint them (not that I could)
though their beauty haunts me.

3. Item

In the doctor's office, an article:
"Scrotum Enhancement: The New Plastic Surgery."
I cross my legs, stricken with empathy,
even though I am a woman.
But what, I ponder, does a beautiful scrotum look like?
We can chart ages of the aesthetics of breasts,
the fullness or leanness of women's thighs, bellies, hips.
We know the summons of the erect phallus,
its ploughs and paraphernalia. But what, pray tell,
truly enhances a scrotum?

4. Testament

Men, Brothers, I want to testify
with something like love.
Let us forget about skyscrapers for a while,
leave the sorry business of convincing and evicting,
forget about the difference between naked and nude.
Let us suffer a change of heart as wide as God's hips,
offer ourselves in trust, swear on our tender parts.
Let us be open.

The Way Between Them

(a curve
   sliver of moon
   slight as a glance
   in the late day winter sky
sun slips past the curve of the planet
like the dress sliding down her shoulders
amber light pooling all
is falling
         falling
she imagines him
a bear become stars
riddled with light
he imagines her
green wind
humming through dark water

this is the way between them
his breath a silver
         O

her dress sliding down
the amber curve of her shoulders
their spines arching)

Still Life

Still Life with Thief

A lit window.
January.

Black tulips in a raku bowl.
A child, her ear on the belly
of an old yellow dog.
The shadow of a woman laughing,
Soundless.

Outside, snow hisses
as it falls.

Water Road

The stone fish in my friend's garden gapes – hungry or amazed.
When we were young, we talked all night, smoke misting

like fine rain. On the island, men bring gifts of fish.
I dive into my grief again, again. The summer it poured,

never rained, the year we almost lost it.
All that weather.

Our children come and go. We empty the old house, catch the
long slant of light by the late winter window: ghost jellyfish moon,

the blue river that tends to the sea, as in *taking care*,
as in *goes by habit*. We talk – cast, reel in, cast.

I walk in the night with my friend, though we are in different cities.
The green air travels with us, charged.

Reunion

I am trying to know the trees of my mother's youth,
the flamboyants of Mauritius I have never seen,
on the other side of the world. In her poem, December
is a celestial monseigneur, languid, afflicted with ennui.
He makes his rounds, trails his purple cloak, *sa pourpre*,
over flamboyant blossoms. His congenital indifference,
his *essentialness*, inflames crowds of swooning blooms
with the fever stain of stigmata.

I know a more modest exotica, the blush
of prairie apple blossoms that breaks your heart
like the impossibly beautiful girl destined to die
of terminal sweetness; the nine days' wonder
of northern lilac I gather in armfuls for the blue jug
before the open window. I know December
in different excess: icelocked, private. Spare
as a thin-lipped preacher's wife, her knuckles chafed
from too much praying, scrubbing, making do.

In the next room, I hear my daughter,
my green girl, fervently colouring
the umpteenth version of her glory bird.
She sits him always in leafless winter trees,
like the skeleton poplar hoarfrosted outside her window,
and blazons him paradisiacal: salmon, fuchsia, magenta.

I move him to the flamboyant outside
my girl-mother's window. The late afternoon room
where she has been reading Rimbaud
is darkened against the day.
She is imagining ripeness.

When she hears the glory bird begin to sing
po-co   a   po-co   po-co   a   po-co
she looks up. I cannot see her face,
but I feel her smile in the textured December heat.

Dreaming of the Dead in the Desert

Some just turn up, ordinary
as a workday morning. Same old.
They seem touched by absence into sharper focus,
but they bear no big news.

A friend arrives, one breasted
and crazy beautiful in a red cowboy hat.
Happiness pierces me.
I tell her if Meryl Streep and Joan Crawford
had a love child, she'd be it.
We laugh till it hurts.

How did your father find you,
middle of Nowhere,
End of the Trail Road, Hope County,
mistaking you for a map home?

All night we burrow into sleep
while the wind worries the camper
like a ship at sea.
The dead lean into us.
The desert and the stars press on
their colossal indifference.
Our hearts stretch wider
than we ever imagined possible.

Thirst

Do you pray? the young priest asks,
his eyes like moving water,
skin smooth as a plaster saint's,
hair the colour of prairie grass when winter leaves.

No rain for weeks.
The blind eye of moon.
The dog a breathing shadow.
My tongue, dumb as veal.

Listening to something that sleepwalks:
Knees scraping the cobblestones of a virgin's shrine.
The singsong rub of beads.
The idea of a God who wants these dry grinds.

A thin shim wedges open a heavy door.
Attention bends, a tuned ear.
Breath that coaxes flame.
A luna moth.
Filament of dragline silk, the smallest snare.
Light breaking. A baby's mouth
at the lull of nipple. The flight path
of a violet green swallow stitching
its colour into air.

First green, then
the knit of bone laid bare.

5 Ways of Listening to a Blizzard

1.

a rabid dog wild
with longing for god
knows what
circles the house
throws himself
at the rattling windows

2.

the starving dead
severed from appetite
wail their phantom hunger
a haunting trick

3.

when the news comes
on the phone
at the door
on the tv maybe
in the middle of an ordinary day
the world tilts
the woman whose child is lost
opens her mouth
centuries of grief

4.

the preacher
seven black feet tall roars
fundamentals
of the End
not fire
this:

5.

how easy
to lie down
in this craziness

easy as curling under
the red quilt
a smell of bread
while the world outside
cracks
open

The Names of Snow

still
in the night's ear
snow repeats its names
to the man whose wife has died

who spends a long time looking
for things
his tongue stretched
to the place of the pulled
tooth

less and less
he goes to the door
drawn to the window
the night field adrift in snow

a stranger in the glass, moving
his lips

Still Life with Pulse

Why this bright morning should I remember
My child stunned to find her small pulse beating,
Then crying "I'm alive!" in the dark of December?

All the crowded days, misplaced, squandered,
All the bills and clocks, the fusted speeding,
Why this bright morning should I remember

Merryn, barely five, eyes charged with wonder
In the moment, hung and trembling – her meeting
"I'm alive!" in the dark of December.

That small rise and fall of blood, that tender
Pulse in the machinery of knowing, fleeting.
Why this bright morning should I remember?

What did I tell her then? How did I send her
Bundled into that cold morning, greeting
"I'm alive!" in the dark of December?

My girl grown, gone, and me in a floundered
Wash of age and love and yearning,
Why this bright summer morning would I remember
Her cry – "I'm alive!" – in the dark of December?

In Praise of Tending

the way you drift to a minor key when you hum
polishing the table your mother rescued
from the haunted house

the way you know without thinking
to bring a cutting of spider plant or wandering jew
to a friend who needs rooting

how you let the cat out
in
out again

cover small plants
against the fray of wind and frost
minister to green
how you attend to blushes,
stutters, quickenings that
pause

command at supper, Look!
how light holds the willow
we planted

the way we lean into the current
of what we remember
of sacraments

the way dust settles in its shadows like debts
carried so long they seem slight as ash

how we come to know *do no harm*
is a kind of stretching

a tendril

Bowl Sings the Blues

I'm empty and waiting, baby,
To beg and to share.
You know I'm empty and I'm biding, child,
I'm ready and I'm clear.
Just bring me your blues, World,
Your rich naked cares.

I'm turned out of wood, boy,
So I know about saws.
I'm spun out of clay, girl,
And I'm versed about flaws.
So bear me your blues, World,
The twist of your laws.

I'll take mush for the baby,
And viands for the king.
Leftovers for the beggar, child,
I'll take roadkill and sing –
Sing it sixteen ways to Sunday
On a hymn or a spring.

They say beggars can't be choosers,
But that ain't all true.
No, beggars just can't be choosers
When you tail the queue.
But if you choose to start empty
What you get's always new.

I'm hollowed and I'm staying, baby,
To ask and to share.
You know space is my tenant, child,
I'm waiting and I'm spare.
Just brood me your blues, World,
Your rich naked cares.

Out of Order. Thanks

says the scrawled sign on the dryer
in the Gila Junction Laundromat. We pace,
waiting for the washer to wind up, time boring
into us, the thrum thrum
of this humdrum zero place.
Thanks for what?
I chew it like a Zen koan.

Meanwhile ... Winter. Off Season.
The high desert rehearses
its declensions of drought,
its economies of scale:
Little Dry Creek. Big Dry Creek.
Arroyo Grande. Arroyo Seco.

> (asked why she painted
> flowers so big, Georgia O'Keeffe
> said, "I'm never asked why
> I paint rivers so small.")

Here we are, strangers
to ourselves and this place, flush
with time and space: *retired.*
I watch our clothes writhe dry, stunned
unbelievably into happiness.

Out of order.
Thanks.

Still Life with Recurring Dream

Apples.

A dog barking.

Arriving in the house of a strange woman
to find my mother's paintings on the walls.

What do you dream about,
I ask the beautiful young woman gambling
at the party of anarchists.
Aging and loss, she answers, barely missing
a beat.

Travelling on the narrow raft
of a borrowed bed,
I have grown young again, so young
I have become my mother's most radiant baby.
I hold myself in my arms, drift anchored.

Stray dogs cache their scrounged food
in the wounds of old trees.
The fruit in my mother's paintings ripens.

What We Mean When We Say Love

Thaw. Unclenching.
A many splendoured _____ (blank).
Part altar, part stage.
A stake. Trophies. Fixes that hold.
A rooted leaning into currents of humming,
ecologies of resonance.
Marriage as real estate.
A good deal. Ace high.
Listening to wind.
The man who said, "During one march alone, nine babies were
born under the fig trees in the middle of storms."
A surge like the sea. Lunge. Plunge.
The woman who said, "We didn't win the war, but I learned a lot "
Revved awake – terrified, estranged – into the lunar translations
of home, the pulsed breathing of those you love.

Small Song for the Old Bed

Bed, your small empathies, warm as soup,
beckon: bosom, bromide,
all that soothes a little while.

Elbow room, estuary, blue raft,
rhythm that murmurs *lap*
                          lap
purls round your plump comfort,
your chummy dogpile snog of the familiar,
pleasant as an egg.

Bed, at day's end,
I want to lie down.

You won't refuse,
your old courtesy easy as you please.

Breath harbour, little willow boat,
carry me gently.

Grand Canyon

At the rim, she wings it.
A twitch of big bang dust, hounded
through the gouged, high noon cathedral, seething.

Darkness swallows light from the bottom up.

Ego, love child of desert rat and turkey vulture,
orphaned in the Great Unknowing,
scritches and circles, sniffing
through the carrion alphabet
for some sounds to speak
to this hugeness.

Awk, says Raven, disappearing.

JANNIE EDWARDS was born in South Africa and now lives and writes in Edmonton, Alberta. Her second book of poetry, *Blood Opera: The Raven Tango Poems,* is a collaboration with visual artist Paul Saturley and has been adapted for the stage by Edmonton's Prosperous Tangueros Consortium. Her videopoem, *Engrams: Reach and Seize Memory,* is a collaborative work inspired by the installation tryptych of Edmonton artist Darci Mallon. The work features Edwards' poetry translated into American Sign Language and performed by Deaf actor and translator Linda Cundy. Jannie Edwards' website is http://www.jannieedwards.ca.